OBAMA THE MAMBA
President of the Slums

by
Kevin Fegan

Playdead Press

Published by Playdead Press 2012

© Kevin Fegan 2012

Kevin Fegan has asserted his rights under the Copyright, Design and Patents Act, 1988, to be identified as the author of this work.

A CIP catalogue record for this book is available from the British Library.

ISBN 978-0-9572859-9-6

Caution
All rights whatsoever in this play are strictly reserved and application for performance should be sought through the author before rehearsals begin. No performance may be given unless a license has been obtained.

This book is sold subject to the condition that it shall not by way of trade or otherwise, be lent, resold, hired out, or otherwise circulated without the publisher's prior consent in any form of binding or cover other than that in which it is published and without a similar condition including this condition being imposed on the subsequent purchaser.

Playdead Press
www.playdeadpress.com

Loosely adapted from the book "Homeland" by George Hussein Obama and Damien Lewis.

Produced by Artbuilding Projects in association with Curve Theatre, Leicester, and The Lowry, Salford. Supported by Arts Council of England

First performed on 12th October 2012 at Curve Theatre.

Special thanks to Paul Kerryson, Fiona Allen and Iain Gillie at Curve Theatre and to Robert Robson at The Lowry and to West Yorkshire Playhouse for early development of the play as part of their Transform 2011 season.

Also special thanks to George Hussein Obama and the people of Huruma, The Huruma Centre Youth Group, the Mwelu Foundation, Damien Lewis, Simon Manyonda, William Simpson, Paul Abbott and Julie Batten.

In loving memory of Sheila Okisa Okoth who passed away during the writing of this play.

www.obama-themamba.com

LOTTERY FUNDED

Kevin Fegan, Playwright and Poet
www.kevinfegan.co.uk
"Britain's most innovative playwright"
(Plays International)

Kevin has written to commission around 50 original stage plays for a wide variety of theatre. Current commissions include an adaptation of "Urban Grimshaw & the Shed Crew" (Bernard Hare) for Pilot Theatre for national tour in 2013.

Recent work includes:
"Slave" - Winner of the Best New Play Manchester Evening News Theatre Awards 2011 & Winner Best Play or Film 2011 Human Trafficking Foundation Media Awards. "Slave" (adaptation of book by Mende Nazer & Damien Lewis) for Feelgood Theatre at The Lowry (2010) and tour (2011).

"Fireflies: a love story waiting to happen" – Nominated for Best New Play Manchester Evening News Theatre Awards 2011. "Fireflies" was commissioned & produced by The Lowry in association with Lioneyes TV (2009).

This is the 7th & 8th time Kevin's plays have been nominated for M.E.N. Awards.

In 2002 he was Winner of Best New Play M.E.N.Theatre Awards for "52 Degrees South"(co-written & co-directed & co-produced with Andy Farrell) at the Imperial War Museum North - a Commonwealth Games Cultureshock commission. His cult rave play in verse "Excess XS" set in Manchester (the first play to use a D.J. mixing live) and "Strange Attractors: love in a virtual world" (the first stage play about virtual reality co-produced with Granada TV) both for Contact Theatre were winners of Best New Play in the U.K. Regions 1992 & 1994 - Plays International.

His early stage plays include his verse play "McAlpine's Fusilier" (1988) and "Game Challenge Level 7" (1993 community play for Moss Side/Hulme at the time of the "gunchester" killings) - both produced by Contact Theatre; also "Private Times" for The Library Theatre Manchester 1990 (and produced by prisoners at H.M.P. Grendon in 2001) and "Rule 43" for Cracked Actors which toured theatres and prisons for two years in 1989-90.

Large-scale site-specific work includes "Lord Dynamite" (co-written with John Fox), a Welfare State International production for L.I.F.T.'91; "The Clay Man" at Upper Campfield Market Manchester (a Manchester City of Drama '94 production) and Woolaton Hall Nottingham (Newartswork) and "Seven-Tenths" for Walk the Plank Theatre Ship (British tour by sea 1996).

Plays for young people include "Get Real" (Blackpool Grand 2003), "Captured Live" (Leicester Haymarket 2004), "The Ghosts of Crime Lake" (Oldham Coliseum 2005), "When Frankenstein Came to Matlock" (Mansfield Palace Theatre 2008), "ABC123"and "The Selkie Boy" (Ashton Theatre at Forum 28 Barrow-in-Furness 2008 & 2009) and "Wan2tlk?" (Liverpool Everyman 2001 and published by Methuen Drama).

Devised work includes Quarantine's award-winning "White Trash" at Contact Theatre Manchester in 2004 and "EatEat" at Leicester Guildhall (co-produced with Leicester Haymarket Theatre 2003).

Community plays include "Not Much Matches Mansfield" for Mansfield Palace Theatre, performed in the town centre (2012), an adaptation of "Love on the Dole" for The Lowry (2004), "Oh W.O.T. A Lovely War" (new version co-written with Andy Farrell) for The Lowry (2006), "Deckchair Tales" for Opera North at Mansfield Leisure Centre (1993) and "Shipyard Tales" for Welfare State International in Barrow-in-Furness (1990).

Studio theatre plays include "Blast" a Manchester Poetry Festival Commission at Contact Theatre (2004), "Totally Wired" (Big Theatre at Contact 2000), "White Van Man" (Ashton Theatre 2002) and "The Forest" (Mansfield Palace Theatre & The Lowry 2008).

Kevin has also written several plays and drama serials for BBC Radio 4, including "Blast" which was Nominated for a Sony Award Best Drama 2001.

Kevin has written & produced several short films and worked as a Storyline Writer for Granada TV's "Coronation Street".

Kevin has published 10 collections of poetry and edited several anthologies and is a regular performer of his own poetry.

Kevin and George Obama

MESSAGE FROM GEORGE HUSSEIN OBAMA

Huruma Centre Youth Group is a registered self-help group with the Ministry of Gender and Youth. It has thirty-five members. It was formed with the aim of creating job opportunities for youths within Huruma. The group involves itself in different activities with the aim of finding a solution for the youths who have been abandoned by the Government of Kenya; that is why most of them have decided to engage in criminal activities and drugs. Some of our young girls involve themselves in prostitution and that has led them to be young mothers, from twelve years of age, and some are affected with HIV/AIDS.

Huruma Centre Youth Group has always focused on engaging the youths of Huruma and its environs in community clean ups and sporting activities, one being the Hussein Obama soccer tournament. We have very talented youths in sports, arts and drama; but because the government lacks the agenda for the youths, they just waste their talents because no one is there to empower and uplift them.

The main activity which helps sustain the Group is garbage collection. We charge a small fee of kshs50 (Kenyan Shillings) from each household. The city council charges us kshs1500 to collect the garbage for transportation to the Dandora dumping site. The profits are divided amongst the group members after we buy sacks for putting in the garbage.

The Government is not concerned at all with the slum. This is where you will find flying toilets, blocked sewers and many things which are inhuman.

Huruma slums is where the saying goes "survival of the fittest" and "do or die" - better die on your feet than die on your knees begging.

Most of Huruma residents were before staying in Nairobi City in makeshift shelters; but were chased away in early 70s and brought to Huruma.

Refugees from Somalia, Ethiopia and Eritrea have invaded the slum and they deal in unknown deals. During the daytime you will not find them, but at night they are mostly found taking khat (miraa) and black coffee. Huruma slums has the biggest goat market in Kenya, here we have about one hundred slaughter houses. Most Nairobi residents come to buy goat meat in Kiamaiko market in Huruma slums. We have had a customer who we later came to know as Mr. Hempstone, the US Ambassador to Kenya. We have also had an opportunity of meeting the former French Ambassador to Kenya, H.E Madam Elizabeth Barbier.

The problem with Kenyan Government is that they won't nurture talents which are available in slums. What they are best in doing is to harass and arrest youths without any proper or meaningful reason. Most of the charges are suspicion of robberies.

During one of the Group's community clean-ups, one member was arrested and charged with being drunk and disorderly. When we went to enquire at the police station we were all arrested with creating disturbances. We were told to part with kshs2000 so that we could buy our release. It took the intervention of the Area Councillor who came to our rescue and we were all released.

Life in Huruma slums can be shocking and terrible to explain. Huruma slums is where you can find yourself being killed or robbed at any time of the day. Youths have no jobs, which makes them decide to engage in crime and girls in prostitution. Huruma slums is the only slum in Kenya which has about thirty girls in jail from different countries for engaging in drug trafficking.

It is just the other day when two young guys were shot by police and a toy pistol implicated on them. There was a passerby who witnessed the shooting and told the whole story to media houses, but no action was done. The cops are still roaming in Huruma and they are still based in Huruma police station.

The slums need a leader who can make life changes and have a lasting solution for the slum dwellers so that they don't have to rely on hand to mouth; but work to have a better life for their children and their grandchildren. One day, God can change the lives of slum dwellers and the world to understand that there is nothing impossible before God.

COMPANY

George Hussein Obama performed by Clifford Samuel

Music – performed by Michael Searl

Writer – Kevin Fegan

Director – Kully Thiarai

Producer – Graham Lister

Designer (Set, Costume & Film) – Shanaz Gulzar

Music Created by – Dom Coyote & Michael Searl

Lighting Designer – Philip Gladwell

Sound Designer – Ben Harrison

Associate Lighting Designer – Richard Owen

Production Sound – Simon Moloney

Stage Manager – Fiona Curtis

Stage Manager – Greg Akehurst

Production Carpenter – Andy Humphreys

Communications Director – Lesa Dryburgh

National Media Officer – Sally Homer

Digital Associate – Bianca Winter

Casting Agent – Sam Jones

Creative Learning Co-ordinator – Jennifer Welwright

Voice of Mother/Auntie Sarah performed by Sarah Niles

"OBAMA THE MAMBA – President of the Slums"
by Kevin Fegan

ACT ONE – FAMILY
THE MAMBA
MY MOTHER
MY OLDER BROTHER
CHRISTIAN
FLYING

ACT TWO – PRISON AND CHILDHOOD
A KIND OF INNOCENCE
ABSOLUTE ZERO
CHANGA'A
AUNTIE SARAH
RUGBY
THE REPUBLIC V OBAMA

ACT THREE – A LIFE OF CRIME
THE LOST YEARS
ROBIN HOOD

ACT FOUR – REDEMPTION AND OUR BARRY
ONE LOVE
OUR BARRY
THE PRODIGAL SONS
OBAMA'S MAMBAS
MR PRESIDENT

ACT FIVE – IDENTITY AND BELONGING
TRIBES
DEAR MZUNGU
QUESTIONS I WANT TO ASK MY FATHER
THE WHITE HOUSE
HURUMA

ACT ONE – FAMILY
THE MAMBA

GEORGE IS A STANDING PASSENGER ON A MATATU

I like "war" – this is what we call fighting.
They call me "The Mamba" because I am fast like the crocodile.
I strike first so they never get away. Always hit them first, knock them down, before they can attack you.
I have been slashed by machetes, gouged by broken bottles, beaten with iron bars, smashed by stones; but no one has put a bullet in me – not yet. You have to prove your "jam" by giving rival gangs a "pano".
I am a one-man crime wave, a badass gangsta. We are 20 - 30 brothers, the Huruma gangstas. We go about our work tooled-up. Welcome to "Nairobbery". My speciality is car-jacking matatus. The economics are simple: a matatu carries maybe sixteen passengers: each with a wallet, mobile phone, jewellery.
The first time I robbed a matatu I was with Ramjo and two others. Ramjo is two years older than me and a trained boxer: a hard man, a dangerous man to cross, but a real joker and a hit with the girls.
We have one pistol between us and I carry it because I have the crazy eyes. The matatu has the words "Street Killer" sprayed down one side. I slide in beside the driver while the others move among the passengers. The driver is blaring his horn to clear a path and blasting reggae music

from his speakers. Matatu drivers are notorious: other vehicles get out of their way. The matatu slows down as we reach the darkest stretch where the streetlamps aren't working and the road is full of craters. I whip out the gun and level it at the driver:

"Stop the fucking vehicle! Pull over, now!" He raises his hands above his head, his eyes wide open. I feel my pulse racing with a mixture of excitement and fear: of my own power, of the risk of being killed, of being forced to really hurt someone. Ramjo and the others are yelling at the passengers and collecting their valuables and cash.

"Don't drive, don't move. If I see you move, I'll shoot you."

Matatu-jacking is a hateful crime. If Kenyans on a matatu catch a thief, they often take the law into their own hands. An angry mob would beat a thief half to death. The police would not intervene. There is no surrender if the police catch you, they have a shoot-to-kill policy. The life expectancy of a gangsta is never very high, but neither is life in the ghetto. Death is usually the only way out.

"Hakuna matata" – no worries.

With money in our pocket, we buy food and go clubbing. We find plenty of "supuu", this is Sheng for pretty girls. The Mamba also has the charm of the crocodile. They say my father was one for the ladies. We smoke weed and drink changa'a until we fall over, K.O. Then back to Huruma ghetto to sleep it off.

MY MOTHER

GEORGE IS WAITING BY THE PHONE TO TALK TO HIS MOTHER.

My mother has had a heart-attack. I am expecting a call from her.

Jael Atieno, was 22 years old when I was born and my father died. He paid three cows as a dowry for her.

She is tall and willowy, like many Luo people. She wears her hair in braids that fall to the small of her back. They sway and dance when she walks. She is a quiet and graceful African beauty.

She was a single parent in Nairobi, working as a secretary in the treasury ministry. When I was six years old, she had another baby, Marvin, named after Marvin Gaye, and a "mzungu" called Christian came to live with us.

My mother was both strict and soft. When I behaved myself, I was lavished in love; but if I stepped out of line, she would beat me with a stick that she kept in the corner of her bedroom. She would order me to lie down on the floor so that she could whack me across the bottom. She would beat me until the pain brought tears to my eyes.

"I'm sorry, Georgie, but you made me do it."

Sometimes, while she was out, I would take her stick and throw it into the bush. When she couldn't find it, she would ground me and I couldn't go out to play.

Age 15, after my first night in a police cell for smoking hash, my mother arrived in the morning to bail me out.

"You are a complete disgrace and a failure."

My gratitude was mixed with shame.

On the way to Auntie Sarah's, she took me to a barbershop to shave my Bob Marley dreads so that I would, at least, look respectable.

At age 17, my mother announced that she was leaving Kenya. Christian had walked out two years earlier and now she was going to work in South Korea.

"Don't you want to know why I'm going?"

"Mum, I can look after myself."

"I'm not leaving you, Georgie; I'm making a life for myself, for all of us. I'll send you money when I can."

I wanted to tell her that I loved her and to ask for a second chance.

During the time I was rotting in prison, my mother married an African-American and moved to Atlanta, in the USA.

The day after my release, I phoned her. I hadn't spoken to her for three years. For the last nine months I had disappeared completely.

"We were worried sick. No one knew where you were. We feared the worst. Why didn't you get a message to me? I'd have found a way to bail you out."

"I'm sorry, mum, but I had to deal with it myself. I didn't want to bring shame on the family."

"You have a little sister now, Chrissie. She is two years old and beautiful; everyone is so proud of her."

"I won't be a lost son any more, I promise."

I have tried to get a visa to the States to visit my mother and Marvin and the little sister I have never seen. When my story was published, I was hoping to do a reading tour and make her proud; but they have refused me a visa. It's not easy to get into the States, especially if you are an ex-offender. Believe me, it's even more difficult if your brother is the President.

My mother has never given up on me. She has never stopped loving me, in spite of everything.

She will call soon, I know it...

MY OLDER BROTHER

GEORGE IS PLAYING FOOTBALL AT PRIMARY SCHOOL.

Our football is made of paper bound with plastic and tied tightly with string – it's not exactly what you'd call "round". It bumps along the dusty ground. I must score a goal before the bell goes for the end of break-time.
A car pulls up outside the gates of Nairobi South Primary School and two figures get out. The ball is dancing at my feet, I am just about to shoot for goal when a teacher calls: "Obama! You have visitors."
I don't want to stop, but I kick the ball across to one of my team-mates. A tall woman holds out her hand. I quickly wipe my sweaty palm on my short trousers.
"You don't recognize me, do you George? I'm your Auntie Zeituni, your father's sister. There's someone very special come to meet you."
I keep glancing back to see if my team have scored.
"This is your brother, Barack; he's come all the way from America to see you."
Where is America? This man looks more like a mzungu than an African. I smile and say nothing. I want to get back to the game. The headmistress tells the visitors they have to leave because they don't have my mother's permission to visit. I quickly say my goodbyes and they leave.

CHRISTIAN

AS A BOY, GEORGE IS HELPING CHRISTIAN PREPARE A MEAL.

This white painted bungalow is our new home. There is a giant TV and the fridge is packed with chilled sodas of every description. I have a bed all to myself.
Christian is fun to have around. He picks me up and swings me around by my arms, like a windmill.
Christian has rented this house for us in a Nairobi district called "Umoja", which is Swahili for "unity". It is an area for well-to-do black Africans. I can't ask my mother why she has a white friend, but I overhear that Christian and my mother met at the office block where they both work.
Christian is the first white person with whom I have any real contact. His eyes are an incredible clear blue, like the sky over our home village after the first rains. He has a kind face, creased with laugh lines. He wears shorts that show a pair of tanned and hairy legs. No African man would be seen dead in short trousers, for they would be a laughing-stock. I touch his hairy arms.
Our house has its own garden with swings and slides; but what really draws my eye are the vehicles parked on the drive. Sandwiched between a Camper Van and a Jeep is the most amazing machine I have ever seen. It looks like a rally car with massive mud-eater tyres. It has a scowling face with a fearsome expression and a big red winch, like a tongue in the monster's mouth. Down each side are the

words "Danger 4 x 4". Wow! It is the coolest machine in the whole of Nairobi.

"Can I sit in it? In your "Danger" mobile?"

True to his word he takes me out for a superfast drive on the open road.

Christian has come to Kenya as an Aid Worker. He visits projects all across Kenya. Whenever he is away, I miss him.

His native language is "French". I thought all mzungus were British, like the white people we learn about at school, who colonized our country. We have language lessons in the kitchen. I tell him the Swahili word for "hello" – "mambo". He tells me the French – "bonjour".

"Thank you/asante/merci".

"No Problem/hakuna matata/pas de probleme".

When Christian is at home, we all speak English. I can beat him at scrabble, but he beats me at chess.

When he cooks, he throws alcohol into the hot frying pan so that it bursts into flames. Why is cooking seen as "woman's work"?

Christian plays rugby. As I watch him making for the touchline, I begin to appreciate why he loves the game. I tell myself, one day, I will play rugby as well as Christian and make him proud of me.

Marvin is not Chistian's real son, but he still calls him "dada". I can't bring myself to call Christian "dad", even though with my Umoja friends I refer to him as my "father". If I start to call him "dad", what would happen if I lost him?

FLYING

GEORGE IS ON A PLANE.

They have published my book in France. I am flying to Paris for the launch.

HE REMEMBERS A CHILDHOOD CONVERSATION WITH CHRISTIAN.

"What is it like," I asked Christian, "Flying in an aeroplane?"
"C'est magnifique."
"How does it feel to be in the clouds?"
"Like you are inside a trick of magic."
"How fast does it go?"
"Faster than your voice."
"How can this be?"
"As you take off, the g-force pins you down to your seat."
"They glide across the skies of Nairobi."
"I'll take you with me one day to France."
"You would do that for me?"
"Bien sur, with your mother and your baby brother."
"How far is it?"
"Eight hours to Paris. Time enough to watch an in-flight movie and enjoy a good meal and fine wine."
"Are all Aid Workers rich like you?"
"Believe me, I am not rich."
"I would like to fly an aeroplane; I'm going to be a pilot one day."

"Pas de probleme."
"I am going to travel the world and earn lots of money."
"Why not? If you study hard, you can do it, n'est-ce pas?"

Whenever we got into a chase downtown, after a street-robbery, we'd head for wasteground where we knew the streetkids hung out. As soon as they saw us coming, they'd point us to a hiding place and swarm around whoever was after us -
"Mister! Mister! Buy me a meal, mister!"
And we would disappear.
Most people in Kenya would prefer it if the "chokora" didn't exist; but not us. There was a brotherhood between the street gangsters and the streetkids. After a robbery we would take those kids who had helped us for a good meal of rice and lentils.
The kid I was closest to was known as "Scram". His dusty, wiry hair stood out at crazed angles, as if he'd just been electrocuted and his clothes were full of holes. He had a big gap between his front teeth and a permanently runny nose which he was always wiping on his sleeve. His bare feet were scabbed and his toenails broken. He had no idea how old he was. One day I brought him some of my old Tonka toys from my mother's house in Umoja. He inspected the toys as if they were a lucky find on the rubbish dumps. He didn't want to play with them, he talked about how much he might get for them and what he would do with the money. Next time, I took some of my old clothes. I gave him a t-shirt with "Hakuna Matata" on the front and an old pair of trainers. He looked like a performer from MTV.

"I feel like a million dollars."

"You know, Scram, there are people living in places like Westlands and Lavington, with gardeners and maids and nurses and nannies and cars and jeeps and swimming pools and private helicopters and they just keep getting richer and richer."

"So how do we get what they've got?"

It was a reasonable question.

"You know what I'm going to do when I'm as old as The Mamba? I'm going to have a jumbo jet and fill it with dancing girls and a casino and a huge swimming pool and the girls will come from America and Russia and China and London and Planet Mars and all of you will be invited because you are my brothers and I'll give each of you loads of "maganji" to gamble in Scram's Casino and I'll throw the biggest party Nairobi has ever seen and we'll fly around dropping empty champagne bottles and cigarette butts and girls' bras and stuff so that everyone will know what a damn fine party we're having up there and the reggae and soul and beat will be blasting out so loud that no one in the city will be able to sleep a wink and behind that plane I'll be flying a huge banner saying "Scram's Jumbo Party – By Invitation Only..."

For as long as I can remember, Shiyayo has lived next door to Auntie Sarah's shack in the Huruma ghetto. Our homes are made of galvanised iron and wood tacked together on a patch of waste ground. Shiyayo lives with her uncle and his children. There are six of them sharing a bed, a sofa and the floor. Shiyayo is dark and petite. I was always asking Auntie Sarah to send me over to her place:

"Auntie, send me across to get some sugar from Shiyayo's uncle."

"But we're fine for sugar, Georgie."

"I know, but send me anyway."

"Why, you're sweet on one of those girls, aren't you? Like father, like son. Well, if you have to, here, go get this bowl filled."

Shiyayo is from the Luhya tribe. She is the last of five children and her father died when she was four years old.

As a young girl, she was taken on a school trip to the airport.

"Look at all their smart uniforms, they are so pretty."

The teacher told her that their jobs took them all over the world. Shiyayo rushed home to tell her mother:

"When I grow up, I am going to become a flight attendant."

At night, Shiyayo would pray:

"Please God, let my limbs grow long like my father's because I have to be very tall to work on a plane as a stewardess."

Shiyayo, Scram and The Mamba...in another story we might all have met in the sky, on an aeroplane among the clouds. Our lives could have taken a different route, to a different world, to another reality...

ACT TWO – PRISON AND CHILDHOOD
A KIND OF INNOCENCE

GEORGE IS IN COURT.

"How do you plead?"
"We would like to speak for ourselves, your Honour. I have been elected spokesperson –
"And you are?"
"Obama, your Honour; George Hussein Obama."
We had been drinking all day in a changa'a den in Umoja – myself, Ramjo, Stevo and Mandeka. It was early evening and there was a squeal of tyres outside. The cops burst in and rounded us up. They took us in their Land Rover to Buruburu police station and charged us with a robbery which had taken place earlier that day. We pointed out that we were drinking all day and that the lady serving us could provide our alibis; but they were not interested.
We have spent a full week in police cells before we are driven to the Law Courts. We are offered a last chance to buy our freedom, but we're pleading Not Guilty. Yes, we're on the game, but we did not commit this robbery so how can they convict us? Conviction for a violent robbery carries a sentence up to fourteen years. In a Nairobi prison that is little short of a death sentence.
"Your Honour, we are pleading Not Guilty to the charges."
"You deny the charges against you?"
"We do, your Honour. We did not commit this robbery so we are pleading Not Guilty."

"Very well, the four accused in The Republic versus Obama and Others will be held on remand until the full hearing. Is that clear, Mr. Obama?"

"It is, your Honour, and thank you, your Honour."

We are taken to the Industrial Area Prison in Nairobi, listed as one of the top ten worst jails in the world.

ABSOLUTE ZERO

THE MAMBA IS WORKING OUT IN THE WASHROOM OF THE PRISON CELL BLOCK.

We are where we are. We deal with it. We survive.
What hits you first is the sheer number of bodies packed into one room. Over a hundred prisoners competing for every square inch of floorspace, baking in the suffocating heat. A ruthless African sun beating down all day long.

You have to establish a routine. We have taken over the toilet block and washroom and turned it into our makeshift gym. Over time the stink becomes bearable. Each week we dream up a new exercise to keep body and soul together.
When I first used this washroom, two big cons followed me in. I had stomach cramps from the lack of food and was unloading my bowels, thinking this is so fucked-up: one minute we're drinking changa'a, the next we're in this hellhole. We could be facing fourteen years. I am twenty years old. Fuck that.
"Where's the new guy hiding his cute little ass?"
I quickly pull up my trousers.
"Come out and pick up the soap, new guy."
I prepare myself to wage war when I hear Ramjo's voice:
"You looking for someone, brothers?"
"New guys gotta learn some respect."
I emerge from the cubicle to see Ramjo, Stevo and Mandeka facing off against two bulky cons.
"Hussein, brother, these guys friends of yours?"

They are much bigger than Ramjo but I've never seen him back down in front of anyone.

"Hussein says he doesn't know you, so get the hell out of here."

"You hear that? New guys ordering us about in our own washroom. This is where we bring our – "

RAMJO KNOCKS HIM OUT.

"Never abuse the crocodile while you are still in the water."

"No one fucks with the Huruma brothers. All for one."

Food is the trigger for everything. The meals cannot keep a grown man alive. Boiled vegetable water and once a week a single chunk of meat. I never appreciated before the power of hunger and what it can do to a man. Hunger breaks men. It destroys their self-respect. Some cons try to kill themselves or are driven insane. Some of the younger men become wives for extra food.

Some of the cons have been on remand here for five years. They are bone thin, like walking skeletons. They have a sunken, desperate look in their eyes from the gnawing pain of the hunger.

"If you could have anything to eat, Ramjo, what would you have? Matoke? Ugali? No, Pilau – every time."

"Stop going on about food, you're just reminding us how hungry we are."

When I arrived the guards asked me for the name of my tribal chief, I said nothing. I will not tell anyone from my family I am in this place.

We send word to our Huruma brothers and they come with rolls of cash hidden in places where the guards would never find it. We are able to buy a prisoner in the kitchen to look out for us with extra rations, until our case is heard before the court.

Celebrations are sweeping the land. After twenty-four years in power President Moi has stepped down and Kenya has a new President Kibaki and his Rainbow Coalition; but corruption is a disease in Kenya. There is more democracy in this cell block than in most of Africa. On the block, it is The Charge who runs things. If you want to buy food, tobacco, weed, pills, he can sort it. The Charge isn't a big guy, but he's smart and he's surrounded by bruisers. There isn't room for fighting so The Charge adjudicates when it kicks off. He's The Man. But The Charge is elected by his cellmates. If he is released or convicted, a new man is elected in his place.

The Loud Mouths are prisoners who lock the rest of us up during the day for the guards. But lockdown is selective. The Charge is exempt because he has to secure deals with the guards. We have made ourselves exempt because we are four and there are not many who will challenge us. Outside the cell block we sit in the fresh air and the shade of the prison walls, as long as we are back in the cell for the seven o'clock roll-call. If the numbers don't add up, there is trouble.

The guards take cons away for private, bespoke beatings. They use bamboo poles and plastic strips to flay you alive. Sometime they beat a man in front of the rest of us as a warning. One lunchtime an old man is demanding his proper portion of sukuma-wikki.
"I'm not moving until I get my fair share."
A baton smashes against his metal bowl.
"Trying to get a double helping?"
The baton crashes against his head with a hollow wounding crack as the bewildered old man falls to his knees. His hands try desperately to shield his face as three guards beat him.
"We'll teach you old man –"
SMASH.
"A lesson –"
SMASH.
"You'll never –"
SMASH.
"Ever –"
SMASH.
"Forget."
SMASH.
A fourth guard takes photos of the beating with his mobile phone.
"Nice work reshaping his face, he was an ugly old dog. There we have it, something to remember him by."
"Damn Ramjo, we've got to change our lives. No way do I want any of this again."

"Brother, there isn't a day goes by when I'm not thinking the same. It's the end of the road, brother, no more fucking around."

"We got to find a legal way to make a living. You seen what this place does to people. End up here again and we're dead men. Once we're out of here, it's the end of the fellowship, brother. "

"It's down to you, Hussein. You're our voice, you got to do the talking to the judge. Anyone can charm us out of this place, it's you. We got your back while you're in here; but you're our only chance of getting out."

"You got any idea what you'll do, if we get out?"

"Working with kids, teaching, maybe. You and me, Hussein, we were always good with the kids."

CHANGA'A

At Mosocho Academy, I join a group of Nairobi kids to form a gang under the leadership of the "Professor". It's Friday night and we are sneaking out of school. Professor is taking us to our first changa'a den. Changa'a is a cheap, illegal knockout brew made from fermented maize and sorghum flour, laced with methanol, brewed by poor people all over Kenya.

The gang has chosen "Hussein" as my street name. There are lots of Georges at school, but no other Husseins. It is my second name and there is something exotic about it.

GEORGE KNOCKS BACK HIS FIRST SHOT OF CHANGA'A.

"Down in one, Hussein! You're the man!"
A few tots later, I am gripped by a sense that I can do anything.
"Another bottle!"
"First, the test."
Professor gets to his feet.
"Before you're allowed the next bottle, you have to pass the test."
"Watch me, I can do it."

GEORGE STANDS ON ONE LEG AND STRETCHES HIS ARMS OUT LIKE A CRUCIFIX AND COUNTS TO TEN.

"One, two…nine, ten!"

"You're a natural, Hussein. Hey, over here, another half bottle!"

"Let's have a show of hands: who blames the whites for all the shit that's happening in our country?"

"If not the whites, who do you blame?"

"I know I have a mzungu father, but no one ever teaches us about the good things the whites have done."

"They did a lot of bad stuff."

"I blame the people at the top who are creaming off billions, while those at the bottom have nothing. People are scared to talk about this shit at school."

"All you can do is drink, innit bro?"

"Damn, you're the man, Professor! You're right, all you can do is drink."

By the time I'm fourteen, we are hitting the changa'a den every Friday night and, when we can afford it, a disco in the nearby town of Kisii on Saturdays, in search of pretty girls.

We speak in our own street language, called "Sheng" – a mixture of Swahili, English and tribal languages. When we speak Sheng, the grown-ups cannot understand us. The teachers beat us if we use it at school.

The night before our exams, we are drinking heavily. It is the last time we will be together as a gang, so we are celebrating the end of an era. When I pass my exams, I will be going to the National School and I will become a pilot.

AUNTIE SARAH

I will not be going to the National School. I will not become a pilot. My mother can see I am troubled and suggests we pay a visit to Auntie Sarah, my father's oldest sister, who lives in Huruma.

Christian drives us there in his "danger-mobile". Minutes from Nairobi centre, the glass office blocks and plush hotels give way to a vista of rickety wooden shacks and stalls. People are squatting on the dusty verges, hawking their wares: blood-red tomatoes, dried fish, worn-out shoes, all manner of second-hand goods. We overtake a man pulling a cart. He wipes the sweat from his brow and I sense the gulf between us. I am a child of privilege, he is one of the teeming hordes of uneducated, underclass who are little better than beasts of burden.

A view of the Mathare slum opens before us: a wide, shallow valley filled with the smoke-blue haze of cooking stoves and smouldering rubbish. Tin, plastic and wooden shacks are piled on top of each other in hopeless confusion. The ghetto draws me in. This is a place of true survivors. If you could live here, with the gangs and guns, the prostitution and drugs, the changa'a dens and open sewers; you could live anywhere.

Affluent Kenyans and white people steer clear of this city of the dispossessed that lay at the heart of the wider capital. Even if I hadn't arrived with a mzungu step-father in a flash car, my blue-black skin, my clothes and my accent mark me as an outsider. The slum-dwellers stare at our danger-mobile, as if it had fallen from a far-off planet, at its mzungu driver and at the black kid with the clean clothes and shiny shoes, the scrubbed nails and the neat hair, who stinks of privilege. This is not the "being different" I crave.

Auntie Sarah rushes out to greet us. I can see how tough her life has been in the lines on her face, the yellowing skin around her eyes and her hard calloused hands. She welcomes us to her home. The compound is surrounded on four sides by walls of wood and corrugated iron. There are a couple of cramped, brick-built rooms, one doubling as a kitchen and the women's bedroom, the other serving as a living-room, with tv and intermittent electricity. There are jumbles of tin huts along one fence for the men and the boys and a tin shack toilet in one corner with a bucket and a tap with running water.

So this is where the Obamas live in Nairobi.

Auntie Sarah asks me to help her sell snacks at her roadside stall. She squats on a stool, cooking deep-frying fish on a charcoal stove. I sit behind the stall, gazing out at the riot of life around me.

"I hear you messed up your exams? Are you giving up on your education?"

"No, Auntie."

"You been misbehaving, Georgie? Is that why you didn't do so well?"

"I've been pretty stupid."

"You know what your father would say if he was alive? He'd tell you you're wasting your abilities. You're a clever boy, Georgie, you're a fool if you squander your talents."

"I'm sorry, Auntie."

"Sorry's no good to anyone. Stuff happens in life that we don't expect. Look at me: whoever would have thought I'd end up here? But I deal with it. A good life can be made almost anywhere."

"I guess."

"But a good education is a rare blessing; it will certainly help."

"Thanks, Auntie."

"You know, Georgie, you've lived a life of privilege. And let's not pretend it isn't because of that mzungu father you have. Most Kenyans would give their right arm for the kind of chances you've been given."

I like it when Auntie tells me how it is. I need this kind of blunt and direct approach. She has seen too much to care what anyone thinks of her. She has refused to accept the kind of laziness and abuse that Kenyan men are sometimes wont to visit on the woman of the household. She is an unapologetic, single woman with a coterie of children around her, making her own way in the world.

I feel ready to open a new chapter in my life and to try again at my new school.

RUGBY

GEORGE IS PLAYING RUGBY.

I am the youngest player in the rugby squad at Dagoretti High School. The climax of the season is the tournament between the top Kenyan schools. This year it is held at St. Mary's, which is mostly populated by elite white kids. It is a mixed school, so there are girls galore in the audience. It is a golden opportunity to show our bravado. Most of the players are 18 years old; I am 15.

I told Christian to come in the afternoon. It is our last match and we have to win. I feel a mixture of panic and pride as I run out onto the pitch. I can't see Christian in the crowd.

The ebb and flow of the match is pretty much equal. I stand on my lonely wing, watching the furious struggle unfold. The ball has yet to reach me. All of a sudden, our side make a break and I see the ball arcing down the line of players until it reaches me. I tuck it into my side and my feet flash across the turf toward the try line. My opposite number lunges at me, but I side-step his diving tackle. I kick out for the try line and drop the ball, slamming it into the hallowed earth. Touchdown!

CROWD ROARS.

My team-mates are dancing wildly around me. I can't see Christian anywhere: the one person I really needed to see me score that try.

A few weeks later, it is half-term, and I return home to Umoja. The parking lot is empty. I hurry inside to my mother.

"Where are the cars?"

She bites her lip and shakes her head.

"But, Christian –"

"Gone; just gone."

How could he be gone? He'd been my father for the last ten years; he couldn't just be gone.

"Gone where?"

"I don't know. Gone for good. Gone."

THE REPUBLIC VERSUS OBAMA

GEORGE IS IN COURT AGAIN.

"The Republic versus Obama: the defendants plead Not Guilty."

GEORGE RAISES HIS HAND.

"Obama, is it? You wish to make a point?"
"I do, your Honour. Am I permitted to speak in English, as the preferred language of the courts? I find it more suitable to express what can be complex arguments."
"Permission granted. You may argue your case in English."
"I'm grateful, your Honour. While I fully respect the process of the courts, I feel I must point out that this case has been going on for nine months and has twice been adjourned –"
"Objection!"
"Over-ruled. Continue Mr Obama."
"Thank you, your Honour. I am not a lawyer, but once again the complainant has failed to make an appearance."
"Objection!"
"Over-ruled. Sit down, Prosecutor. I trust you are following Mr Obama's arguments? A fine thing to hear such a command of English, don't you agree? Continue, Mr Obama."
"Thank you, your Honour. Once again, I fail to see any of the police present or witnesses. It begs the question, what

serious effort is the Prosecutor making to progress his case."

"Objection, your Honour!"

"Mr Prosecutor, I'd be most interested to hear upon what basis you wish to object?"

"Your Honour, I can assure you the complainant will be here at two o'clock sharp to give evidence."

"And do you think the court should wait for the man to deign to put in an appearance?"

"Your Honour, I crave the court's indulgence…"

"This repeated failure to present a case makes a mockery of the court process."

"I'm sorry, your Honour, but …"

"Continue Mr. Obama."

"Thank you, your Honour. Your Honour, it is myself and my co-accused who are suffering at the hands of the Prosecutor's inability to bring a case against us. How much longer can this go on? I presume it is within your power and that of the courts to dismiss this case. It seems to me there is no justification in keeping us locked away any longer. Justice and Liberty are important concepts and they should be respected and valued by all concerned."

"Your Honour, I must object -"

"You will do nothing of the sort. Back in your seat. I have heard the arguments. By the authority vested in me by this court, the case of The Republic versus Obama and Others is dismissed. These men will be released under section two-one-zero of the Kenyan Penal Code."

ACT THREE – A LIFE OF CRIME
THE LOST YEARS

AT AUNTIE SARAH'S IN HURUMA.

"Think you can choose the life of a loser and get away with it? Your mother has told me all about your night in the police cells."
"Auntie, it was only smoking 'stoot'."
"This is no laughing matter, Georgie."
"I'm sorry. Things started going wrong when Christian left."
"Then get a grip, there's no excuse after all you've been given in life. You're an Obama, Georgie; so act like one."
This time I stay at Auntie Sarah's for two weeks. She arranges for Roy, my father's first-born and head of the family, to visit me. Roy is happier being known by his Muslim name – Malik.

AT THE MOSQUE.

"It's good to know who you are, Hussein. It's the faith of our father, the old man's religion."
It's a Friday, the Muslim Holy Day, and Malik has brought me to the Jamia Mosque in downtown Nairobi.

THEY PERFORM "WUDU": THE RITUAL WASHING OF HANDS AND FEET BEFORE PRAYER. GEORGE IS UNCOMFORTABLE AND FEELS UNDER-DRESSED FOR THE OCCASION.

"You know how to pray, Hussein?"
"Some."
"If you get lost, just follow what I do."

THEY SPREAD THEIR MATS ON THE FLOOR, FACING EAST.

I am struck by the silence and the stillness.

LIGHT STREAMS IN THROUGH THE HIGH ARCHED WINDOWS.

I never imagined that, in the heart of this heaving city, such calm and peace could exist.
I want a miracle to happen. If God shows himself, I will accept him as my father. But I feel nothing. The mask of the teenage rebel falls across my face once more and the moment is lost.

GEORGE JOINS HIS GANG.

I have been expelled. I'm hanging out with older Umoja kids who have already quit school. We fill the emptiness of our days listening to music, drinking changa'a and smoking "stoot". I have the clothes, the walk, the talk and the attitude. I watch "Pulp Fiction" and "Scarface". I want to be a badass gangsta.
In the evening, we work as matatu touts – the callers who recruit customers onto the buses. We earn about three dollars a night and spend it on changa'a. What we really

need is maganji – "real money"; so we resort to pickpocketing and mugging. We are the "Magnificent Seven", the sons of the fast and angry city.

OUTSIDE GEORGE'S SHACK AT AUNTIE SARAH'S COMPOUND.

My mother and Marvin have gone. Our Umoja home has been closed for good.
I am seventeen years old. I have a new girlfriend who lives in Umoja. She is a pretty slip of a thing from the Kamba tribe. She is a great party girl and a dancer to die for. Her favourite club is "New York", in downtown Nairobi. She tells me to my face what a crap dancer I am, whenever I try to keep up with her moves. She has a great sense of humour and knows how to take me down a peg or two.
Auntie Sarah reaches out to me once more. She has built a couple of new one-room shacks in the compound and offers me the key to one of them, telling me I can stay there whenever I am in need of sanctuary.
"You're still an Obama. No one will ever disown you here."
The shack is very basic, but vastly superior to the makeshift shelters I share with Scram and the other streetkids.
Huruma is a dangerous place, but the ghetto doesn't feel alien to me anymore.
I want to prove I can thrive in the ghetto. I set about drawing my Umoja gang into Huruma. The only way to make ourselves known is to up our game and prove ourselves in battle.

Shots ring out as the police charge into the slum, chasing a thief who has fled into Huruma to try and lose them in the dark alleyways. The thief is wide-eyed with terror as he vaults across open sewers. A woman steps out of the shadows into his path and a policeman's bullet strikes her in the stomach. She clutches her wound and crumples to the floor. We pick her up, hoist her high above our heads and rush her to the nearest clinic. We throw a handful of bloody banknotes at the staff.

A crowd gathers, chanting for revenge against the police. Shots are fired over the crowd. The incident fuels my rage against the authorities and drives me to execute more robberies in a vicious circle of injustice. My lost years begin.

ROBIN HOOD

THE MAMBA IS COUNTING HIS TAKINGS FROM THE NIGHT BEFORE.

When I was a schoolkid, I saw a cartoon of Robin Hood. It struck a chord with me. Kenya needs a Robin Hood, as England needed one in those days.
In Huruma, kids die of hunger or simple curable diseases while the big men in the suburbs live a life of luxury, funded by corruption. Society is rotten, just as it had been under England's King John.
Is it really so bad for us to steal from those who have, to feed those who have nothing? At least there is some kind of karma to what we do. When we do something bad, we do something good: we steal someone's wallet, we buy these streetkids a meal.
One day a girl called Rachel asks for my help. She is a pretty thing about twelve years old. A couple of years more and she will likely be a "shangingi", a working girl. She tells me her nine year old brother is desperately ill. Her mother is dead and her father is a changa'a addict. She is the head of the household. I know she is telling me the truth. Even in the ghetto, people don't lie about such things. In fact, beneath the desperation, there is an honesty that is breath-taking. I give her a thousand shillings, about fifteen dollars.
Her brother has typhoid, a fever all too common in the ghetto. She gets him to the hospital just in time. She buys maize flour and other basic foodstuffs for the family. Her

father takes fifty shillings for changa'a. I don't blame him. God only knows what a life he has led. The rest she gives to the doctors.

"Keep my brother alive."

SCRAM SHOWS UP.

"Hey, Scram, where have you been, kid?"
"I was picked up by a "charity". They promised me food and shelter and an apprenticeship. I was shown how to hit a nail with a hammer. Then, every day, we made furniture. I was learning nothing, for no pay. It didn't take me long to realize I was better off on the streets. Wow! Where did you get all the money?"
"We met a very generous man last night, with 64,000 Kenyan Shillings in his pocket - over a thousand dollars. He was as drunk as a skunk, pulling out his fat wad of notes, like the big man, and buying all the girls a drink. "
"A thousand dollars! Damn, I'm gonna be just like you guys when I'm grown."
Sometimes, after a robbery, I wonder if the person we have mugged deserved it?
He was probably going to use the money to pay a relative's hospital bill or his kid's school fees. You never get to any of the fat cats with their chauffeur-driven Mercedes and their bodyguards, their gated compounds ringed with electric fencing and razor wire.
If I was President, I would rule like Robin Hood.

ACT FOUR – REDEMPTION AND OUR BARRY
ONE LOVE

GEORGE IS DRIVING A MATATU, WITH BOB MARLEY BLASTING THROUGH THE SPEAKERS.

Prison was not for me. A life of crime is behind me now.
I am driving a matatu when I can, to earn a little cash to survive. Believe me, the irony is not lost on me. Scram is my tout, recruiting passengers for me - I'm setting a different example these days.
Drivers christen their matatus with names that reflect their style: "RoadRage" or "Weapon of Mass Destruction". Mine is called "One Love". People think I named it after Bob Marley's song, but I named it after "Pendo Moja", which also means "One Love". Pendo Moja is a self-help slum organization set up to support the young people of Huruma. We work with the youth to try and provide an alternative to a life of crime, prostitution, drug and alcohol abuse. I am only twenty-three myself; I still drink and smoke a little weed and I can't afford to backslide. Working with the ghetto kids helps me keep on the straight and narrow. The Huruma ghetto took me in when I was at my lowest ebb, showing me its compassion. Now I want to give something back.
But there is another reason I joined "Pendo Moja" and that is Shiyayo, the girl next door I had grown up with at Auntie Sarah's. Shiyayo is more like a sister to me than a lover.

Our first project is cleaning up the garbage dumps that double as informal toilets. We take kids on house-to-house garbage collections, charging each household fifty shillings a month – less than a dollar. The recyclable waste we sell to dealers, a rare source of income for slum children. Sometimes children turn up for garbage patrol and they can hardly stand they are so weak with lack of food. We fetch them a plate of rice and lentils and tell them to join us when they feel stronger.

I realize the difference between myself and the slum dwellers: I have family contacts. I have been given a second chance; most in the ghetto have never been given any chance at all. Everyone in the ghetto needs help and we know a favour will be returned. With homes so closely packed together, fire is a big risk. If one home burns, the fire could sweep through the ghetto like an inferno. We have no one to rely on but ourselves.

On one occasion thick black smoke billowed out of a neighbour's place. The neighbour was out at work so we smashed down the door and formed a human chain, passing buckets of water to douse the flames. I stood at the front of that chain with Rajab's niece, Mwanaisha, who had recently come to live with us in our Huruma compound. By the time we finished, we were completely exhausted, our clothes and faces blackened with soot and smoke. His home was a scorched and stinking mess, but at least the structure had been saved.

The people in the slums care for each other in ways the outside world has no concept of. In the generosity of those who have nothing, I realize the ghetto has a lot to teach the wider world, if only it would listen.

I see a young man get on board the matatu. He is wearing battered jeans and a t-shirt and he has the "crazy eyes". I see him signalling to friends at the back. I know what's coming next:
"Pull over! Pull over now or I'll shoot you in the head!"
I want to say to him, "I know, I've been there; but this isn't the answer."
But I also know it will make no difference.
I pull over as the passengers hand over their valuables.

OUR BARRY

GEORGE IS FALLING TO SLEEP WATCHING TV AT AUNTIE SARAH'S.
SHE GIVES HIM A NUDGE.

"You should be watching this, Georgie – it's your big brother in America: Barry has become a Senator. An Obama as a Senator in the U.S.A."
"That is pretty damn cool."
"Your father would have been proud of his American son."
"If he can make it, well, you never know…"
"It's good to hear you talking like that, Georgie. You really have changed. I'm proud of you too, you know that?"
I wondered what it would be like to see each other now? Sure, we are brothers, but we are worlds apart.

THERE IS A GUNSHOT NEARBY.

A notorious policeman, nicknamed "Killer", has shot a young thief in the leg. We know him as a slum dweller who is too soft for a life of crime, a layabout but no villain. Killer yells at him to walk to the police station. The young man stumbles to his feet and drags his wounded leg along. A crowd gathers, angry and threatening. Killer shoots the young man in the other leg and the crowd rush forward; but Killer points his pistol at them and yells into his radio for backup. The wounded man falls behind a tree with a makeshift light attached to it. The young man holds both hands up, begging for his life. Killer bends forward and places his pistol against the young man's head. For a second, the crowd holds its breath until Killer pulls the trigger and blows the guy's head apart in a shower of blood and brains. Killer fires again over the crowd to drive us back. Reinforcements arrive and tape off the "crime scene". The police take out an old jacket and place a pistol in the inside pocket, then place the jacket over the dead body. They want us to see how powerless we are in the face of their death squads; they want us to see they can do anything to us and get away with it. In the ghetto, we are deprived even of the right to life. The Mamba in me resurfaces and wants to wage war; but how, in the face of such horror and injustice?

THE PRODIGAL SONS

AT THE OBAMA COMPOUND IN KOGELO.

This is my first visit to Mama Sarah's place in Kogelo, a small village in rural Western Kenya. It is a typical Luo homestead. Mama Sarah is the grandma I share with my American brother. It is Spring 2006 and Senator Barack is visiting Kenya. He is already there with dozens of Obama relatives, the U.S. Ambassador and other dignitaries.
Barry is unmistakeable: tall, lean, bronze skin with close-cropped hair. He projects an air of confidence.
 "George, isn't it? It's good to see you again; it's been too long."
"Yeah, it's George; it's good to see you too."
"How have you been over these last twenty years?"
"I never forgot you."
"Gee, it's good to see the little brother of the clan."
Barry introduces me to his wife and family.
"So, how are you keeping, George? I hear it's been tough?"
"Yeah, I'm trying to catch up on some of what I've lost."
"But you're doing good now?"
"You know, you're a big inspiration to me. You kind of helped me turn my life around."
"Thanks, George, that's good to hear. I never forgot you either – that little kid at primary school playing soccer."
"You remember that?"
"Sure I do, I wrote about it in my book."
"That's right, I've read it."
"You did? What d'you think?"

"Well, truthfully, I read it a couple of years ago to find out more about our father."
"So, did you learn much about him?"
"Enough to know that I'd have liked him to be alive when I was growing up."
I leave Kogelo with a mixture of emotions. I feel closer to my brother, but I failed to raise the issue of Africa's dispossessed in the slums.

OUTSIDE A NAIROBI HOTEL.

Back in Nairobi, I receive a message that Barry wants to meet me again. I go to the Serena Hotel, not exactly a hangout for those from the Nairobi slums. There is a moment at the hotel entrance when the guards refuse me entry; but when they learn who I am meeting, I'm whisked inside. I run into my big brother in the lobby. He is surrounded by security.
"George, it's good to see you again, but listen: I got to rush to a meeting. I've got two days in Nairobi, I'll call you. We can arrange a time to meet and have a proper talk, okay?"
"Okay, I'd like that."
The call never comes. Someone in the family "forgets" to fetch me. There are those who believe that I have shamed the good name of Obama and am not suited to meeting an American Senator. I feel certain that Barry wouldn't judge my fall from grace.

OBAMA'S MAMBAS

ON THE FOOTBALL FIELD.

Shiyayo, Rajab and a few others decide to set-up our own community organization: the Huruma Centre Youth Group.
As well as the garbage collection, we run arts and crafts workshops, tae kwando classes, talent competitions and a Miss Ghetto beauty contest. I coach the football team: Huruma Centre F.C. - "Obama's Mambas".
I use the Obama connection around the time of the U.S. presidential elections to sponsor the team with a new football strip and the team become known as "Obama's Mambas".

IN THE DRESSING-ROOM AT HURUMA F.C. BEFORE THE BIG MATCH.

My fellow citizens, the task before us is great.
Before we consider that task, let us remind ourselves of how far we have come. There have been many sacrifices along the way. We acknowledge the debt we owe to those who came before us. They said this day would never come. They said our sights were set too high. They said our community was divided, too disillusioned to ever unite around a common purpose. But on this day, at this defining moment in our history, we have done what the cynics said we couldn't do. We are one team and our time has come.

Ten years ago, no one thought we could even play football. Our position was to stand and watch others, to pay for the glory of others. Now we are the players.

We started out barefoot. People laughed at our patchwork strip. Yet we still won some of our matches. The more times we put the ball in the net, the more the opposition and their supporters stopped laughing. Time and again we showed our potential. Now we have brand new boots, a brand new strip, and we are on the verge of success. We are Huruma F.C.

Those who still doubt us are on the wrong side of history. We have emerged from the Huruma ghetto. We are no longer fearful, we are fearless. We are no longer shameful, we are proud. We remain a young team, but the time has come to put away childish things. We have come of age.

Today we have to go out there and beat our arch rivals, Sports Connect. Victory will be ours today. We will be Nairobi Super League Champions.

We will send a powerful message that change is coming to world football. Some of our players are already being selected for the national team. One day our players will play for Manchester United and Barcelona, A.C. Milan and Bayern Munich.

Starting today we begin the job of rebuilding this community. There was a time I was a ghetto criminal. I lived for drink and drugs, for women and money. Our success brings opportunities. For our brothers and sisters to be educated. For our families to prosper. These are also our goals.

We have always had hope. Hope is the thing inside us that insists, despite all the evidence to the contrary, that something better awaits us, if we have the courage to reach for it, to work for it and to fight for it. Hope is what led a band of people to rise up against an empire, what led a generation to heal nations and free a continent. Hope is what led us here today. The belief that our destiny will not be written for us, but by us, by all those men and women who are not content to settle for the world as it is, who have the courage to remake the world as it could be.

We are the people of the Huruma ghetto. We are amongst the poorest people on earth. But we are also Huruma F.C., "Obama's Mambas", and we are champions.

MR PRESIDENT

GEORGE IS WATCHING TV

Barry's face begins to appear all over Kenya. Our "long-lost son" is running for President of the U.S.A. Apart from a few close family and friends, I haven't told anyone that I am his youngest brother. A European journalist makes contact. I show her around our Huruma home and let her take photographs. I tell her I am happy living in Huruma and about the good work we are doing here. I also tell her I am proud of my brother's success. When the article appears, she writes about tracking down the U.S. presidential nominee's brother to a shantytown, where he survives on less than a dollar a month. Even here, you can't live on a dollar a day, let alone a month. The headline tells how "One aims for the White House while the other lives in an African slum."

I refuse to talk to the media again. I am offered an interview on CNN. Rajab advises me to take the opportunity to have my say because it's a live programme and my story can't be twisted. Things start to change. The "London Times" publishes an interview with the headline, "Life is good in my Nairobi slum."

The U.S. election is an extraordinary event in Kenya. The Obama clan gather in Kogelo. We listen with pride to his victory speech.

AN ARCHIVE CLIP FROM BARACK'S INAUGURAL SPEECH:
"Hope – hope is what led me here today. With a father from Kenya, a mother from Kansas and a story that could only happen in the U.S.A."

We celebrate for days. I send Barry a message of congratulations:

"To my brother, the new man in the White House".

ACT FIVE – IDENTITY AND BELONGING
TRIBES

GEORGE IS WALKING ALONG THE STREETS OF THE SLUMS.

This is where a man was stoned to death in the riots. President Kibaki claimed victory in the 2008 elections and a second term of office. There was anger over claims of vote-rigging. Kikuyu were pitched against Luo. The violence was a nightmare in the slums. Many slum-dwellers spilled over into the Kenyan Airbase; but the military drove them back. Over a thousand people have died in Kenya from the riots and half a million have been displaced. "Wat en wat" – kinship is kinship; blood is thicker than water.

Here, in Huruma, the violence wasn't as bad. Many of us refused to get involved. My wife is Kikuyu, Clyde's wife is Luo. As Clyde says,

"Would I kill my own wife?"

Rajab says:

"There are only two tribes in any country: the rich and the poor."

DEAR MZUNGU

GEORGE IS PLACING LETTERS IN ENVELOPES.

Dear Mzungu,
I am wishing to provide my son with an education; but I cannot afford school fees. Send money.

Hojambo Mzungu (Hello White Man),
I am top footballer. You live in the U.K. Arrange for me an apprenticeship with Manchester United F.C.

Mzungu,
I am a good Christian. Clear my overdraft. My account details are as follows…

Habari Mzungu (Welcome White Man),
Welcome to our country. I have a business proposal. Send money.

Odiero (White Man),
My sister died from malaria. I wish to become doctor. Arrange for me to study in Great Britain.

Dear Mrs Mzungu,
My dream is to own a red dress like the one you wore when you visited my country. Is it possible with your help for my dream to come true? Inshallah.

Hey Mzungu,
I am African rapper. When can I record Number One hit.
Karibou (You're welcome).

Mr Mzungu, sir,
Do you like Kenyan women? Are they not beautiful? I have list of women and young girls, all shapes and sizes; they would like to be wife of a mzungu. Send $10 for catalogue.
Your servant.

Dear Sir,
Send £1 for food so my children can eat today.

GEORGE LAYS DOWN THE ENVELOPES.

People always want to know – does he send me cash?
If not, why not? I think you will find that he has a family of his own to care for, a country to look after, a world to watch over. My brother is not my keeper.
I look after myself. I have a family of my own: a son, Shamil, and a beautiful wife, Razia. Shamil is my son from my first marriage. He lives in Huruma with his mother; although I often bring him to my flat in Umoja. It is true that, from the sales of my book, I have a nice flat in Umoja. I could stay there; but I choose to spend my time with the people of the slums.
Of course, it is also true that I trade on the good name of Obama. A long line of journalists and writers come to find me. They see what they want to see; they write what they

want to write. Some of them come here with money in their pockets from those who wish to dishonour my family name and to use me as a weapon against my brother. They want to rob me of my dignity. So I take their cash – as much as I can get. I drink their mini-bars dry and make them pay for meals for all my friends.

If they are interested in me and not my brother, I offer them hospitality. My wife will make them a meal. If they are interested in our slum community, my friends will be their friends, and my neighbours will show them how we truly live.

QUESTIONS I WANT TO ASK MY FATHER

GEORGE IS IN A POLICE CELL. A GATHERING CROWD CAN BE HEARD OUTSIDE THE STATION.

Apparently, the police and the Kenyan authorities don't like the way they are portrayed in my book. Corruption is a dirty word – even for the corrupt. As Barry says, "Corruption in Kenya is a crisis." It has been estimated the average urban Kenyan pays sixteen bribes every month.
The cops picked me up outside the Jonsang Bar in the ghetto. They have "found" weed on me – how convenient. I told them:
"I don't smoke weed any more – ask anyone."
They are trying to teach me a lesson; but this time it's their turn to learn.
The cavalry have arrived and they are at the gates of the police station.
There is no "big brother" come to defend me; no "message" from the White House; no drones come to bomb the station; no Navy Seals to spring me from captivity; just the people of Huruma, led by "Obama's Mambas", Huruma F.C., demanding my release.

THE CROWD CHANTS HIS NAME.

There are three questions I want to ask my father:
1) Am I A Disappointment To You?
I know that "Barack" means "blessing". How come he got the name Barack and I got George? If Barack is your blessing, am I your curse?

Did your father approve of you? You were expelled from school like me; but your father beat some sense into you. You were fired from your government post as an economist and yet you played your part in the making of modern Kenya.

How was your life with my mother? We had so little time together as a family.

I cannot visualize you. I was only a few months old when you died. I wish for something connected to you. Aunt Sarah once showed me a photo of you holding me as a baby. We have the same ears. Is that love in your eyes for me?

2) Do You Believe In God?
They say Grandfather Obama converted from Christianity to Islam.

There are three generations of Muslims on your father's side.

In Islam you can have more than one wife. In Luo tradition you can have up to five wives. You had four wives. Does this make you Muslim or Luo?

I was brought up a Christian and yet you named me George "Hussein" Obama and my brother Barack "Hussein" Obama?

You declared yourself an atheist when you went to study in Hawaii.
Barry is a Christian.
I am a Muslim.
We are all Luo.

3) What Is A Man Of Principle?
My cousin Rajab says you always had a natural affinity with the underdog.
In 1955, age 19, you were arrested as a Mau Mau sympathizer.
You were the first Obama to be educated. You won a scholarship to university in Hawaii and went on to gain a PhD from Harvard.
You worked for the Kenyan government as an economist.
There are conspiracy theories about your death – there are those who think you are a political martyr.
These are the actions of a man of principle.

And yet you were also stubborn like your father.
You were a womanizer.
I was your eighth and last child. I know I have brothers and a sister here and abroad. Are there any more children we don't know about?
They used to call you "Mr. Double-Double" because you always ordered two double whiskeys in one glass. You were drunk the night you ran your car into a tree in Nairobi and died.
These are the actions of a fool.

Am I living up to your expectations or making up for your mistakes?

What principles should I teach my own son, Shamil?

THE DOOR OF HIS CELL OPENS AND HE IS FREE TO GO.

THE WHITE HOUSE

GEORGE IS DRINKING HEAVILY.
HE IMAGINES VISITING THE WHITE HOUSE.

This is a damn fine house you have here, bro'. A palace, in fact. Man, you could fly a plane through here.
They told me to come to the Blue Room because that's where you receive guests. I bet there's every colour room in this White House, every colour of the rainbow. The President is certainly a man of colour.
Do you like a drink, Barry? I like a drink. I know what they say about me. You and me, we should get hammered one night. I'll supply the Tusker beer if you supply the cognac – is it a deal? Do you know the word "safari" means "journey"? We should go on a little trip together, around Africa and around the West; a little sight-seeing tour of how the other half lives.
I think you should have met me in the Oval Office, where you meet your advisors; because I have some advice for you.
When you think of Kenya, what do you see? Masai warriors? Safari animals? Mount Kenya? You know the people of Kenya as great runners. You say it's because we live at high altitude; because we have to run ten miles to school and ten miles back every day; because we have "legs like birds"; because we have to run for our lives. Let me tell you, I am lean, but I loathe cross-country. I cannot run a long way to save my life.

You know our ghettos from your TV screens: the shit running through our streets and our homes, the children scavenging on rubbish dumps, a people sick with Aids. You think in order to survive we have to block out compassion and love. Let me tell you, "Huruma" means "compassion".

When you think of Kenya, you think of corruption. It is true that there is always a need for money to get anything done in this country. Think of it, for a moment, not as a bribe, but as a "tax". Do you not have to pay a "tax" on your food and clothes? On your cars and your fuel? On your homes and your businesses? On your hospitals and your police? On your rubbish and your old age?

You call us corrupt while your politicians claim for second homes they don't live in, for bills they don't pay; your bankers cream the profits from pensions that are not paid and receive bonuses from banks that have been saved from collapse by tax-payers' money. Your I.M.F. think they can fuck the chamber maid like they fuck the Third World… and you call us corrupt.

Look in the back-streets of your own towns and cities and you will see children sleeping in shop-doorways, look in your derelict buildings and you will see people who need medication and care; look in the bins behind your restaurants and you will see the hungry; look in the dark alleys and you will see people waiting for their next fix. You have natural resources in your country; you have talent; you have infra-structure, education, healthcare, insurance, human rights. Why is it so that you have all these problems? Are you lazy people? Are you greedy people? Ruthless people? No. But still you cannot solve your own problems – why? Do not weep crocodile tears for Kenya; weep for yourselves because you should do better with what you have.

Me and you, Barry, we are like two sides of the same coin. Ying and yang. I am dark and you are light. I am Chuck Berry to your Elvis.

You were twenty-one when I was born, so you've had a head-start. The world has yet to see what becomes of me. I am thirty years old. I could become the voice of Africa's slums or I could become an alcoholic.

People expect so much of us, they can feel let down. They can blame you for losing their job, their son, their wife, their dignity. There are those out there who resent us for what we have become. Just the other day, this guy in a bar starts on me with:

"So you're the big man, Obama; well you don't look so important to me."

Before I know it, we're fighting and I'm dragged back to being The Mamba all over again. The police can pick me up any time, frame me on some weed or robbery charge and I'm going down and never getting out. Someone, somewhere, Barry, wants you dead. They're plotting your assassination as we speak. We could both be killed for what we are, what we represent.

What do you think, Barry? Is it an accident of birth that you were born in the States and I was born in Kenya? Could I have done what you have done? Could I have become President? Could you have done what I have done? Could you have become "The Mamba"? Could my story have been a story of success? Could your story have been a story of redemption?

My brother has risen to be the leader of the most powerful country in the world. In Kenya, my aim is to be a leader amongst the poorest people on earth.

HURUMA

AT A MUSLIM FUNERAL.

"The ancestors are always watching," my cousin Rajab once told me.
When I was released from prison, I went to him for advice.
"The best time to plant a tree is twenty years ago; the second best time is now."
Rajab told me it was never too late to change. I asked him how he felt about my fall from grace?
"Who am I to judge anyone?" he replied, from behind his little round spectacles. "But there are those in the family who will."
After Auntie Sarah's death, Rajab came to live in the little tin shack where I had lived, during my troubled times. Rajab's neice, Mwanaisha and her young son came to share our Huruma home. Now Mwanaisha is also dead.
What was the cause of Mwanaisha's death? She was a young mother, aged thirty-two. How can this be? We will never know. There is no money for post-mortems here. People die every day in the slums.
Muslims bury their dead before sundown on the day of their death. The Muslim cemetery in Nairobi is a beautiful garden at the end of a dirty road, littered with vehicle repair workshops and scrap metal dealers.
A white pick-up truck arrives. Mwanaisha's corpse is in the back, wrapped in a blue blanket. The men unload her body onto a metal stretcher and take her to the holy place. We file in, one at a time, and circle the body anti-clockwise.

She is dressed in a white shawl. Her eyes are exposed. A few prayers are said. The men bury the dead. We are stripped to the waist, digging a resting place for Mwanaisha, when the heavens open and there is a torrential downpour. Rain at a funeral is regarded as a blessing from God. We are well-blessed, slipping and sliding on the moving earth beneath our feet. We finish our task and leave so that the women can pay their respects.

AT THE OBAMA COMPOUND IN HURUMA.

Back at the Obama compound in Huruma, it is flooded with rain. We shovel the rain onto the street, while the women cook huge vats of pilau rice and goat-meat stew. After we have eaten, the women look after the children while the men settle down to drink gin and play scrabble. There is no electricity today so we play by candlelight.
Ramadan is a big powerful man who skins goats for a living. He offers to share his weed with us, but I only smoke cigarettes these days. We call this weed "domm". In many languages, "dom" means "home".
Clyde works when he can, teaching tae kwando, clearing garbage and making jewellery from copper.
Robert was a street kid; now he's studying for a degree at Nairobi University.
Willis was a soldier in the Kenyan army for 12 years.
Aden is team captain of Huruma F.C.
Deangory always arrives with a woman on his arm. He refers to his women as tortoises.

My neighbour Julia, known as "Mama Africa", refers to men as hyenas. She runs a local shop, selling sweets and printed cloth with her own designs. I lay down my final word at scrabble. I spell out "d-o-m-m" to win the game and we all roll around laughing.

We move on to another neighbour on "Obama Street", Caroline, lives in two rooms with her mother, her grown-up daughter, her teenage son, and Richard, a young man who they adopted when he grew too old for the Barnardo's Home and had nowhere else to go.
Caroline's mum, Sheila keeps the family going by brewing changa'a. All around the compound there are plastic containers. People drop in for a quick tot of changa'a.
This is not what outsiders expect an illegal changa'a den to look like; but it is the reality of life in the slums. A neighbour drops in with some friends for changa'a and conversation.
"I am an old man now and lucky to be alive."
He is fifty-four years of age. His name is Kevin Keegan. He tells us again how he was named after a famous footballer who played for Manchester United. I am a Chelsea supporter, but I am able to put him straight, one more time, that Kevin Keegan played for Liverpool.
Caroline has prepared ugali for us to eat. She offers water to wash our hands.
My little boy, Shamil, joins us.
This is where I am alive, in the Huruma ghetto. These are my people.